JOURNEY OF LIFE

Marriage

Ronne Randall

WAYLAND

First published in 2015 by Wayland
Copyright © Wayland 2015
All rights reserved.
1 3 5 7 9 10 8 6 4 2
Dewey number: 203.8'5
ISBN: 978 0 7502 9654 0

MIX
Paper from
responsible sources
FSC® C104740
FSC
www.fsc.org

Produced for Wayland by Calcium
Design: Paul Myerscough and Emma DeBanks
Editor: Sarah Eason
Editor for Wayland: Katie Powell
Picture research: Maria Joannou
Consultant: Sue Happs

Wayland is an imprint of Hachette Children's Group
Part of Hodder & Stoughton
Carmelite House, 50 Victoria Embankment
London EC4Y 0DZ

Printed in China

Alamy Images p. 35 (ArkReligion.com), p. 24 (Brianindia), pp. 18, 22 (Gary Roebuck), pp. 42, 43 (Liquid Light), p. 39 (Maciej Wojtkowiak), p. 32 (Wherrett.com); Corbis p. 14 (Andy Aitchison), p. 20 (Charles & Josette Lenars), p. 13 (Reuters), p. 25 (Stringer/India/Reuters); Dreamstime pp. 4, 8, 23, 26, 29, 37B, 41; Istockphoto pp. 5, 7, 9, 10, 11; OnAsia p. 37T (Luke Duggleby); Photographers Direct p. 31 (Christine Osborne Pictures), p. 40 (Missy Davis Jones Photography), p. 21 (Rosina Redwood Photography); Photos.com p. 34; Rex Features p. 15 (Israelimages), p. 33 (Robin Anderson); Shutterstock pp. 6, 12, 19, 28, 36; Still Pictures p. 17 (Dan Porges); World Religions Photo Library p. 38 (Claire Stout).

Cover photograph: Shutterstock (f9photos)

An Hachette UK company
www.hachette.co.uk   www.hachettechildrens.co.uk

Contents

What is marriage?

$\mathcal{R}$ites of passage are the ceremonies and rituals people have created to mark times of great significance and change. They are like signposts, marking the most important places on our journey through life. Marriage is one of these significant times. When young people marry, they leave the protection of their homes and families in order to set up a home together. Marriage announces to the world that they are now adults, ready to go through life as a couple and perhaps start a family of their own.

Marriage has existed in every human society, and goes as far back as recorded history. People have made laws about marriage in order to ensure the rights of both partners, and to protect the children that are born into the new family. Today, in the western world, many people see romantic love as the best basis for choosing a marriage partner. This was not always so. Until the 20th century, most people married for economic or family reasons. In cultures where arranged marriages are common, economics, education and social standing are still seen as important factors in choosing a partner.

Many Hindus marry a partner chosen for them by their parents.

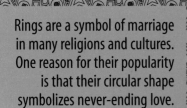

Rings are a symbol of marriage in many religions and cultures. One reason for their popularity is that their circular shape symbolizes never-ending love.

Because of the importance of marriage, most cultures have developed elaborate ways of celebrating the event. These celebrations involve special ceremonies, customs and rituals, and include special clothes, foods and symbols. Following these customs and rituals is thought to bring good luck to the couple.

This book will look at how marriage is celebrated in six world religions: Christianity, Judaism, Islam, Hinduism, Sikhism and Buddhism, along with some secular customs. There are many differences in the way these religions approach marriage – but there are many similarities, too. These show just how universal the experience of marriage is.

FOCUS ON:
Wedding rings

Wedding rings are usually made of a precious metal such as gold or silver. This emphasizes the preciousness of marriage – but there is a historical reason for their value, too. In the past, a ring was also a monetary gift from the groom to the bride. The more valuable the ring, the more the man was seen to value his new wife, and so the higher her status.

In some countries the wedding ring is worn on the right hand, but in much of the world the wedding ring is worn on the fourth finger of the left hand. The ancient Greeks and Romans believed that this finger contained the 'vein of love' that went directly to the heart. In the 16th century, the new *Book of Common Prayer* (1549) in England formalized the custom of wearing wedding rings on this finger by including it in the wedding service.

Double-ring ceremonies, where rings are exchanged by the couple and not just given by the groom to the bride, became common in the second half of the 20th century.

Preparing for marriage

Christians believe that marriage is a gift from God, so it is important to be married in the sight of God. Christian marriage, which is sometimes called holy matrimony, is a sacrament, or a form of worship that connects the participants to Jesus Christ. For all these reasons, Christian weddings take place in churches, and are conducted by a priest or minister.

However, a priest has not always been part of the Christian marriage ceremony. Until the mid-16th century, Christian couples could marry simply by stating their vows before witnesses. At that time, marriages generally took place in people's homes. When new religious laws made it necessary for a priest to conduct a marriage service, the ceremony was moved from the home to the church.

Christian marriages are usually preceded by an engagement, a time when the couple have announced to the world that they intend to get married. As far back as the 12th century, engagements in England and Scotland were made known by publishing the 'banns' in the bride and the groom's local churches for three Sundays in a row. 'Banns' comes from an Anglo-Saxon word meaning 'to summon'. The banns are still read out in Anglican and Roman Catholic churches today.

Diamonds, traditionally seen as the strongest and most precious stone, are now the most popular stone for engagement rings.

A hen night marks the bride's last night as a single woman. Only female friends and relatives of the bride are invited to the hen night.

The bride-to-be is usually given a ring by her fiancé, which she wears on the wedding ring finger. Engagement rings became popular in the 13th century, and were originally plain metal, but gradually it became popular to add gemstones.

Shortly before the wedding takes place, the couple, their families and the members of the wedding party may have a rehearsal, to go through the order of service and make sure everyone knows what will happen. This may be followed by a rehearsal dinner – a sort of pre-celebration before the wedding itself, and an opportunity for the two families and sets of friends to get to know each other.

FOCUS ON:
Stag and hen nights

Some pre-wedding rituals are reserved just for the bride and groom. In western Europe and North America, a man about to be married may have a 'stag night' or bachelor party with his male friends. The group goes out on the town, drinking and having fun, to celebrate the man's last few days or hours of 'freedom'. The stag night is a cultural rather than a religious custom. It dates back to ancient Greece, when soldiers would feast and toast a comrade who was about to be married.

A 'hen night' for the bride – when the woman goes out with her female friends – is a very modern invention that is becoming more popular. In the United States, bridal showers are still more common than hen nights. These are parties where the bride's female friends and relatives gather to 'shower' her with gifts of things she will need for her new home.

7

The marriage service

There are three main branches of Christianity – Roman Catholic, Protestant and Eastern Orthodox – and for each one the marriage ceremony differs in small ways. But all Christian weddings include prayers, hymns, and readings from the Bible, as well as blessings by the minister or priest.

Christian brides often wear white to symbolize purity.

In some Anglican (a branch of Protestantism) and Roman Catholic weddings the ceremony might be a Nuptial Mass, in which the bride and groom receive Holy Communion; or there may be a simpler ceremony, with readings and prayers but no Communion. In Eastern Orthodox weddings, the bride and groom generally take Communion the morning before the wedding service.

The wedding party assembles in church at the altar. Generally the priest or minister enters first, with the groom and the best man. Organ music is often played as first the bridesmaids come down the aisle and then, accompanied by her father (or both parents), the bride walks down the aisle to meet the groom.

In Eastern Orthodox ceremonies the bride and groom exchange rings three times and receive the priest's blessing. In other Christian ceremonies the bride's father may be asked to 'give away' the bride. This custom dates back to a time when daughters were considered the property of their fathers, who transferred ownership to their new husbands. Nowadays it is a symbolic act, a sign that the bride's family approves of her new husband. Today, when many women have independent lives before marriage, some brides choose not to be 'given away' at all.

After hymns sung by the congregation and some words about marriage from the priest, the couple say their vows and exchange rings. In Greek Orthodox weddings, where rings have already been exchanged, crowns are placed on the bride's and groom's heads at this point, and they are given a cup of wine to share. This is to remind them of the story of the wedding at Cana, at which Jesus turned water into wine.

After a blessing from the priest or minister, the couple are declared married. As joyful music plays, they walk hand in hand back up the aisle as husband and wife.

In their vows, Christian couples promise to love and look after each other, and to remain faithful to each other.

Wedding celebrations

Outside the church, well-wishers shower the bride and groom with paper confetti or flower petals. In pagan times, cereal grains were sprinkled over the couple to ensure their union was fruitful. Later sweets, or confetti in Italian, were substituted for grains; gradually these were replaced by the bits of paper we call confetti today. In America and some other countries rice is still thrown.

A reception usually follows the wedding ceremony. This is a party where guests share food and drink, and toast the bride and groom to wish them happiness in their new life together. The toasts and speeches are led by the bride's father, followed by the groom and the best man, and perhaps other friends and family.

Some Christian couples light a unity candle as part of their wedding celebration. The bride and groom each hold a lit candle, and with them together light one single candle, to symbolize the joining of their lives. Members of both families then light a candle to represent the joining of the two families. This North American custom is becoming popular in other parts of the world.

Wedding celebrations almost always include dancing, as well as gifts for the bride and groom. Greek Orthodox weddings combine gifts and dance with a 'money dance', where guests pin money to the couple's clothes as they dance together.

Historically, rice was thrown at newly married couples to wish them prosperity, luck and fertility. Confetti has taken the place of rice in modern weddings.

It is tradition for the bride and groom to cut the first slice of wedding cake together at their wedding reception.

The wedding cake is traditionally cut by the bride and groom together. The couple may feed each other a piece of cake, to symbolize that they will now look after each other's basic needs. Traditional wedding cakes have three tiers, a fashion that was introduced in 17th-century France. In western Europe, fruitcake is the most popular wedding cake, with the fruits and nuts symbolizing sweetness and fertility.

With the party still going on, the newly married couple may leave for their honeymoon, a holiday when they can relax after the excitement of the wedding and spend time together. Before the bride leaves, she may throw her bouquet over her shoulder for one of the unmarried female guests to catch. According to tradition, the woman who catches the bouquet will be the next to marry!

MODERN DEBATE:
MARRYING ABROAD

Weddings are becoming increasingly elaborate and expensive. In 2007, the average cost of a wedding in the United Kingdom was £18,500; in the United States it was more than $30,000.

Many people feel that their wedding day is the most important day of their life, so are happy to spend a lot of money celebrating it. Other people think spending a lot of money on a wedding is too extravagant, and inappropriate for a couple starting out together. They are choosing instead smaller, simpler weddings abroad, with only a few close friends and family.

Do you think it is extravagant to spend a lot of money on a wedding, or do you think this important day should be celebrated in style?

Blessing a marriage

*I*n Judaism marriage is a *mitzvah*, which means a good deed or commandment set forth in the Torah. The Torah, also called the Five Books of Moses, is the Jewish holy book. In the first book of the Torah, 'Genesis', God creates Adam then says, 'It is not good that the man should be alone; I will make a help meet for him.' In creating Eve as Adam's help meet, God made the first marriage.

The Torah – the Jewish holy book. Calling an Ashkenazi bridegroom to read from the Torah is called an *aufruf*, which means 'calling up'.

Jews live all over the world, and their wedding customs often reflect those of the local community. Within Judaism, however, there are two main cultural strands: Ashkenazi Jews trace their heritage to Germany or eastern Europe, while Sephardi Jews have their roots in Spain, North Africa or Asia. All Jews follow the same religious laws, but Ashkenazi and Sephardi traditions can be very different.

Jewish weddings can be held any day of the week except Saturday, which is the Jewish Sabbath. A week before the wedding, as part of the regular Sabbath service, an Ashkenazi groom is given the honour of being called to the reading of the Torah. He recites a blessing before the Torah is read, and another after the reading is complete. After he says the final blessing, the congregation may throw sweets at him, to symbolize a sweet life for him and his bride.

It is considered an honour for the groom to read from the Torah a week before his wedding.

Sephardi grooms are called to the Torah a week after their wedding, and in addition to saying the blessings they read the passage in the Torah (Genesis 24: 2–14) in which Abraham asks his servant to find a suitable wife for his son, Isaac.

For Orthodox, or very observant, Jewish brides, whether Ashkenazi or Sephardi, the most important pre-wedding ceremony is a visit to the ritual bath known as the *mikveh*, to purify themselves for their wedding day. A Sephardi bride may be accompanied by her female friends and relatives, who later dance with her and share an all-female feast.

In some Orthodox communities, it is traditional for the couple to fast from sundown on the evening before their wedding. Many couples, however, no longer follow this practice.

MODERN DEBATE:
FASTING AND THE MIKVEH

Orthodox Jews fast before their wedding day to make the day similar to Yom Kippur, the Jewish Day of Atonement. On this day, Jews fast and ask God to forgive their sins of the preceding year, so that they then begin the new year with a pure heart. In the same way, the bride and groom are expected to fast before their wedding day in order to enter their marriage in a state of purity. This is also why the bride visits the mikveh before her wedding.

Traditional Orthodox couples follow these rituals, believing that they are a core part of their faith. Liberal Jewish couples feel that these rituals are outdated practices and not in keeping with modern life.

What do you think?

The marriage service

*J*ewish brides wear white to symbolize their purity. They also wear a veil, to show that they are as modest as Rebecca, one of the matriarchs, or mothers, of the Jewish people. In the Torah, it says that when Rebecca first met her future husband, Isaac, she 'took her veil and covered herself'.

A Jewish bride's veil is lifted so her groom can see her face. The veil is then replaced and the marriage ceremony takes place.

The groom wears a suit and usually a prayer shawl known as a tallit. The origin of the tallit is in a biblical commandment that the children of Israel should 'make fringes in the corner of their garments, that they …may look upon it and remember all the commandments of the Lord.' (Numbers 15:37–39). The groom's head is covered, with either a *kippah* (skullcap) or a hat. A reminder of God's presence above them, the kippah is worn at all times by Orthodox Jewish men, and during prayers and solemn occasions by less strictly observant men.

Before the ceremony, the bride and groom sign the wedding contract, known as the *ketubah*, in front of witnesses who also sign it. A veiling ceremony called the *badeken* follows. The groom lifts up the wedding veil to see the bride's face, then replaces it. This comes from the story in the Torah of Jacob, who was expecting to marry Rachel. At the last minute, Rachel's father tricked Jacob by putting her older sister, Leah, in her place. Because Leah's face was covered by her wedding veil, Jacob did not realize he was marrying the wrong sister.

As the groom stamps on the wine glass, everyone cries 'Mazal tov!', which means good luck.

The wedding ceremony itself takes place under a canopy called a *chuppah*, which is supported by four poles. Many couples choose four friends or relatives to hold up the poles of the chuppah, which represents the roof of the home the couple will make together.

Some Jewish brides follow an ancient tradition, in which she walks around the groom seven times, to protect him symbolically from harm or evil.

The rabbi begins by blessing the couple, who then share a cup of wine. The groom places a ring on the bride's right index finger and says, in Hebrew, 'Behold you are consecrated to me with this ring according to the Law of Moses and Israel.' The bride may give the groom a ring as well, but this is often done later, after the ceremony. She will also move the wedding ring to the fourth finger of her left hand. The rabbi then reads the ketubah and recites the *Sheva Berakhot*, or Seven Blessings. The bride and groom share another cup of wine, then the groom stamps on the wine glass. Bride and groom are now husband and wife.

FOCUS ON:
Breaking the glass

There are many theories about the origins of this custom, which has existed for many centuries. Some say that it was done so that the noise would frighten away evil spirits. The most widespread explanation is that it represents the destruction of the Holy Temple in Jerusalem in 70 CE, and serves as a reminder that even in the midst of joy we should remember there is sorrow in the world.

Parties and honeymoons

After the ceremony, the bride and groom spend some time alone together, in a part of the marriage service called the *yichud* (Hebrew for 'together'). If they have fasted, they now break their fast with cake and wine.

By the time the couple return to their guests, the wedding party has already begun. There is a meal which begins, as all Jewish festive meals do, with blessings over wine and *challah*, a braided loaf of rich bread, which is broken up and shared among the guests. The food is likely to be kosher, in keeping with Jewish dietary laws, and there are speeches and toasts to the bride and groom.

After the meal, the traditional Jewish grace is sung, and the Sheva Berakhot are repeated, sometimes by close friends and relatives.

Sacred text

Grant perfect joy to these loving companions, as you did to the first man and woman in the Garden of Eden. Praised are You, O Lord, who grants the joy of bride and groom.

Blessing 6 *of the* Sheva Berakhot

The meal is followed by music and dancing, usually including the joyful Israeli folk dance called the *hora*. If the couple is strictly Orthodox, men and women do not dance together.

During the dancing, the bride and groom may be seated in two chairs, representing royal thrones, which are then lifted into the air by several male guests, and held in the middle of a circle while the other guests dance around them. The bride and groom each hold one end of a handkerchief, signifying their connection to each other. This is an Orthodox tradition that has been adopted by many Liberal Jewish couples.

It is considered a mitzvah to bring joy to a couple on their wedding day, so guests consider it a privilege to dance in front of the bride and groom. Some may perform acrobatic stunts to make the dancing even more entertaining.

After the party, the bride and groom may leave for their honeymoon or they may delay this for a week in order to enjoy a bit more celebrating at a series of dinners held by friends and relatives.

Israeli folk music is usually played at Jewish wedding parties. Orthodox Jews may include only Jewish music, while Liberal Jews often include other types of music too.

FOCUS ON:
Seven days of blessings

In some communities, the honeymoon is postponed for seven days, another custom derived from the story of Jacob and Rachel. After he married Leah, Jacob worked for his father-in-law, Laban, for seven years to win the hand of his beloved Rachel. To commemorate those seven years, many Jews continue the wedding celebration for seven days. During this week, friends and relatives of the newly married couple hold a festive meal for them each evening, at which the seven wedding blessings are recited. This round of festive meals is known as Sheva Berakhot, after the blessings themselves.

Arranging a marriage

Muslim marriage is not seen as a primarily romantic relationship. Instead, it is viewed as a social contract that benefits both partners – and that carries rights and responsibilities for both husband and wife. Therefore, in traditional Muslim families, marriages may be arranged by the bride and groom's parents, who are seen as the best judges of who will be a good partner for their son or daughter. However, children are free to reject anyone by mutual consent if they are not happy with the choice of partner.

Although many Muslim marriages are arranged, legally Muslim men and women may also arrange their own marriage, without the help of their parents. In most Muslim communities, once a suitable match has been agreed on, the man must give his future bride a gift, known as *mahar*, which is usually money or gold. This is done so that she will have property of her own.

Along with giving the bride gold and money, the groom's family may also buy her wedding outfit.

Beautiful patterns are worked into the *mehndi* design used to decorate a bride's hands.

FOCUS ON:
Mehndi

The mehndi ceremony can last for two days and is accompanied by music, dancing and festive food. It is traditional for the mothers of the bride and groom to make the first applications of henna on the bride's palm, to symbolize her own mother's love for her and her future mother-in-law's acceptance of her into the family. The woman who applies the rest of the mehndi is usually an unmarried close friend or relative. Sometimes the groom's initials are worked into the designs, and the groom is meant to look for them on the wedding night.

In many communities the giving of mahar happens as part of the engagement; in others it may be part of the wedding ceremony itself.

A few days before the wedding, in a ceremony combined with a party, the bride has her hands and feet decorated with mehndi (henna) designs. Female friends and relatives on both the bride's and groom's side take part in the festivities.

19

Nikah: the marriage service

There are Muslim communities all over the world, each with its own traditions and practices. A Muslim wedding in India, for example, might be very different from one in Morocco, Egypt, Malaysia – or the United Kingdom. As with all religions and cultures, local traditions play a part in how weddings are celebrated. Asian Muslim brides – in India or Pakistan, for example – generally wear bright colours, especially red or pink, which are traditionally associated with joy and good fortune. North African and Middle Eastern Muslim brides usually wear white.

Muslim weddings may take place in a mosque or in the bride or groom's home. If it is in a mosque, the ceremony is usually conducted by a Muslim religious leader called an *imam* or by an elder of the mosque called a *qazi*. Marriages can, however, be performed by any Muslim man who is respected by the community.

The marriage ceremony itself is called the *nikah*, an Arabic word that refers to the relationship between a man and woman and the actual contract of marriage. The guests take their seats first, then the bride and groom enter, attended by their *walis* ('guardians'). The walis, usually the couple's fathers or other male relatives, act as representatives for the couple. In very observant families, men and women sit separately, and the bride and groom are separated by a curtain to protect their modesty.

Red is one of the most popular of wedding dress colours among Indian Muslim brides. Brides also usually wear beautiful gold jewellery on their wedding day.

This Muslim bride is signing her marriage contract in the presence of her witnesses. A Muslim couple sign their marriage contract before the marriage ceremony is completed and they are declared husband and wife by an imam.

The imam may give a sermon on the subject of marriage and the bride and groom's duties to each other. Once he has made certain, in front of witnesses, that the bride and groom are both entering the marriage willingly, he reads some passages from the Qur'an, the Muslim holy book. The bride and groom, and their walis, then sign the marriage contract before the imam and in the presence of witnesses. This is followed by more readings from the Qur'an and blessings and prayers for the newlyweds, their families, and for the entire Muslim community.

Then, because he is now a husband and part of the family, the groom may go to the women's section and offer gifts to the bride's female relatives. Two families, as well as two people, are now joined.

Sacred text

And among His Signs is this that He created for you spouses from amongst yourselves, that you may dwell in tranquillity with them, and He has put love and mercy between your hearts.

Qur'an, 30:21

21

Celebrations and a new life

A Muslim wedding is celebrated with a marriage banquet called a *walima*, which comes from an Arabic word meaning 'to assemble'. In Muslim tradition, marriages must be declared publicly, and the walima is a joyful way of doing this.

The meal may be modest or fairly elaborate, depending on the customs and traditions of the community. In strictly observant families, men and women sit separately. All food is *halal* – suitable according to Muslim dietary laws, which do not allow pork – and there is no alcohol, which is forbidden to Muslims.

After the meal, the bride and groom sit together for the first time as man and wife. They are given a place of honour on throne-like chairs, and their guests sprinkle them with flower petals and rice: fertility symbols that are meant to ensure that they will be blessed with children. The guests present the couple with gifts and money, too, to give them a good start in their new life together.

A Muslim husband and wife arrive at the walima. Walima celebrations are held to publically announce that a marriage has taken place.

The Muslim holy book, the Qur'an. When a Muslim bride goes to live with her husband's parents, her mother-in-law holds the Qur'an over her head as she enters the house, to welcome her into the family.

On their first night as a married couple, the groom may go to his bride's parents' house, but they sleep in separate rooms. If the bride has a brother, the groom may share a room with him, otherwise he sleeps alone. The next morning, the bride's parents give him gifts, and in the afternoon his family comes to escort the newlyweds to their home. Traditionally, Muslim brides go to live with their husband's parents, though this is no longer true for many modern couples. If a bride does go to live with her husband's parents, her mother-in-law is there to greet her when she enters her new home.

For Muslim newlyweds, celebrations may continue for days. A few days after the walima and the *rukhsat*, the groom's family may hold another party and celebration meal in their home, to bring both families together – showing yet again that for Muslims marriage is between families as much as between the bride and groom.

FOCUS ON: Rukhsat

Leaving her parents and her home, especially after the excitement of the past few days, can be an emotional experience for a Muslim bride, and there are often many tears as she says goodbye to her family. In a ceremony known as rukhsat ('departure'), the bride's father gives her hand to her new husband and asks him to take care of her. Amidst more tears and wishes for happiness and good luck, the bride leaves her childhood home as a married woman.

Finding a partner

*A*ccording to Hindu belief, life is divided into four *ashrams*, or stages. Marriage begins the second stage, called the *Grihastha Ashrama*, or 'householder stage', when a man and woman set up a household and begin a new family.

FOCUS ON: Horoscopes

Hindus may consult horoscopes – charts showing the positions of the stars and planets when a person was born – at many key stages of life, including marriage. When a marriage is being considered, the astrologer will make sure that the couple's horoscopes are harmonious; their horoscopes are also used to choose a favourable day for the wedding.

Hindu astrology is derived from the Hindu holy books known as the Vedas. It is related to the Hindu concepts of reincarnation, the belief that after death the soul is reborn in a different body, and karma, which holds that everything we do will affect us in this life or a future one.

Marriage is considered the most important *samskar*, or sacrament, of Hindu life. It is a step that must be taken if an individual is to grow spiritually and achieve his or her potential, and it is a solemn commitment made for life. Traditionally, Hindus see choosing a partner as too important to leave to the couple themselves, and many Hindu marriages are arranged by the couple's families, often with the help of elders in their community and astrologers. They take into consideration factors such as education, social and economic standing, and compatible horoscopes. The future bride and groom must both approve of the partner chosen for them, or the marriage cannot take place.

It is customary for friends and relatives of the bride to bring cakes and sweets for her mehndi celebrations.

Once a suitable partner has been agreed on, an official betrothal ceremony takes place. The future groom and his family go to the bride's house, where prayers are said. The girl's parents then formally announce to the groom that their daughter is promised to him in marriage. The groom's mother may give the bride gifts or money to welcome her into the family.

A traditional drum, called a *dhol*, is played at Hindu wedding celebrations.

Later there may be a ceremony at the groom's home, at which the bride and groom exchange betrothal rings and the bride's father formally accepts the groom as his future son-in-law. Once the ceremonies are complete, the betrothal becomes a sacred contract that cannot be broken.

Wedding celebrations begin well before the actual ceremony. A few days before the wedding, friends and family gather at the bride's house for the mehndi ceremony, at which her hands and feet are decorated with henna designs. There is a party atmosphere – the house is decorated with flowers, and food and treats are served.

A day or two later, at an evening gathering known as a *sangeet*, both families get together for a festive meal accompanied by music, singing and dancing. The rejoicing has begun – and will continue for days to come!

A sacred marriage

On the wedding day, the bride and groom's families meet just outside the wedding venue for the *milni* ('meeting'). Here they exchange sweets and gifts, and embrace to show their happiness at the joining of the two families. In the past, it was customary to hold the milni several days before the wedding. Today, as many communities live farther apart, it is held just before the ceremony.

The entire Hindu marriage ceremony takes place before the sacred fire.

Hindu brides generally wear a traditional sari, most often in red, a colour associated with good luck and fertility. They also wear a great deal of gold jewellery. They may have several wedding outfits and change them often during the day. The groom wears a traditional Hindu tunic and scarf, and a turban.

Inside the wedding venue, the groom is led to a decorated canopy called the *mandap*, where he is given a welcoming drink made of milk, ghee, yoghurt, honey and sugar. The priest blesses the couple, who exchange flower garlands to symbolize their acceptance of each other.

The priest then lights the sacred fire – all Hindu life cycle events take place before a sacred fire, which represents the mouth of the Hindu god Vishnu and symbolizes happiness and enlightenment. The priest recites sacred mantras in Sanskrit, the ancient language of the Hindu sacred texts.

Sacred text

With our first step, may we provide for our
household with food that is nourishing and pure.
With our second step, may we develop our
physical, mental and spiritual strength.
With our third step, may we increase our wealth
by righteous and proper means.
With our fourth step, may we acquire knowledge,
happiness and harmony.
With our fifth step, may we be blessed with strong
and noble children.
With our sixth step, may we live long lives.
With our seventh step, may we be true companions
and remain life-long partners in our marriage.

Saptapadi *or* **Seven Steps**

As she holds the groom's hand, the bride steps over a small stone, showing her willingness to overcome the difficulties they may face in their marriage. Together, the couple walk around the sacred fire four times, throwing offerings of food – usually rice and ghee – into the flames. As they circle the fire, they ask for God's blessings and promise to be loyal to each other and to love and care for the children they hope to have.

The priest then makes a 'marriage knot' in the couple's garments, tying together the groom's scarf and part of the bride's sari. Hand in hand, the couple take seven steps together, reciting a vow at each step. After this they sit down together – now as husband and wife.

FOCUS ON:
Tilak

After the milni, the bride's parents welcome the groom by applying a red mark known as *tilak* to his forehead. This mark shows that the groom is fit and ready to enter marriage, and that his status has changed from that of a betrothed man to a bridegroom.

The red paste used for the tilak is called *kum-kum*. It is made of turmeric and lime powder, which turns the yellow turmeric bright red. In traditional Hindu medicine, turmeric wards off evil and negative feelings. The tilak is applied to the middle of the forehead to symbolize the 'third eye', which is believed to be the centre of wisdom.

27

Joining a new family

$\mathcal{N}$ow that the bride and groom are husband and wife, the groom's mother welcomes the bride to the family by giving her a necklace called a *mangla sutra*. This shows her status as a married woman, and symbolizes protection for the life of the new couple.

Wearing *sindoor* represents the bride's wish for a long life for her husband.

To symbolize the bond of marriage, the groom applies a red powder called *sindoor* to the parting in his new wife's hair. If she is ever widowed, she will remove the dye.

As a gesture of love and respect, the newlyweds touch their parents' feet, and then the priest's, to ask for their blessings. The groom then blesses his new bride, and asks all the guests to do the same. Along with the blessings, the guests shower the couple with flower petals to wish them luck.

Now the bride and groom join their guests at the joyous wedding feast – their first meal of the day (many traditional Hindu couples fast on their wedding day). Family and friends offer gifts and good wishes to the newlyweds, who are treated like royalty.

When the party ends, it's time for the bride to leave with her husband for his parents' home. Some Hindu couples do live with the husband's family, but even if she is not going to live with her in-laws, a new Hindu wife must be symbolically welcomed into their home by her mother-in-law.

On her wedding day, a virtuous bride is said to be like *Lakshmi*, the Hindu goddess of beauty, virtue and prosperity.

Before leaving, she says a tearful goodbye to her own parents and brothers and sisters. She is leaving them for a new life as part of her husband's family, and though there is great happiness, there is sadness as well.

When the couple arrive at the groom's home, his mother is already there to greet her new daughter-in-law. Traditionally, she must enter with her right foot first – this will bring luck to her and her husband in their new life together. At the groom's house, the newly married couple play a game of Aeki-Beki. This game is played by placing a ring and several coins in a tray of water, which is coloured by sindoor and milk. It is said that the person who finds the ring four out of seven times will rule the household. The day concludes with prayers to God asking for love and happiness for the couple.

FOCUS ON:
Lakshmi's footprints

In some Hindu families, the groom's mother greets the bride with a dish of red dye. As she enters the house, the bride dips her feet in the dye and makes footprints on the floor. The footprints she leaves are said to mark the presence of the goddess in the home.

A blissful union

For Sikhs, marriage is an important way of serving God and helping to improve the human condition. By finding individual happiness in marriage, couples add to the happiness of all of humanity. In fact, the marriage ceremony itself is known as *Anand karaj*, which means 'blissful union' in the Punjabi language of northern India, where Sikhism began. The Anand karaj was introduced by Guru Amar Das (1479–1574), the third of ten Gurus who led Sikhism in its first 200 years. The fourth Guru, Guru Ram Das (1534–81), wrote the wedding hymns known as the *Lavan*.

Sikhism sees all people as equal, so marriage is a union of equal partners based on love and shared interests. Dowries, or bridal payments, are forbidden, because marriage cannot be a business transaction, and the costs of the wedding are to be shared as equally as possible between the families of the bride and groom.

FOCUS ON:
The five K's

The Sikh sword and bracelet given to the bridegroom at the *kurmai* are two of the five symbolic items that Sikhs are expected always to wear, to remind them of their religious duties. They are worn mainly by men, but many Sikh women wear them as well. The five K's are:

Kesh: uncut hair, which symbolizes obedience to God by not interfering with nature.

Kangha: a wooden comb for the uncut hair.

Kachera: white shorts worn under clothes, to symbolize purity and modesty.

Kara: a steel bracelet – the circle symbolizes eternity, and the steel represents strength.

Kirpan: a symbolic short sword that reminds Sikhs always to fight for the truth and defend the weak.

Because Sikhs regard it as the parents' duty to find partners for their children, Sikh marriages have traditionally been arranged, if the couple themselves agree. Nowadays, in modern Sikh communities men and women may choose each other, then ask for their parents' approval.

A formal engagement ceremony, called a *kurmai* or *shagun*, may be held at the home of the groom. The bride's relatives give the groom gifts, including a Kara (a symbolic steel bracelet) and a Kirpan (a symbolic sword). The Kara and Kirpan are two of the 'five K's' worn by Sikhs (see box). The gifts are presented in the presence of the Guru Granth Sahib, the Sikh holy book. The groom's parents give the bride gifts as well, often including a dress and gold jewellery. The ceremony includes prayers and hymns, followed by a meal shared by both families.

A few nights (or sometimes weeks) before the wedding, girls and women from both families get together for a night of mehndi, music and food. The bride's hands and feet are painted with henna designs; her close friends and relatives may get their hands decorated as well. Some believe the darker the mehndi patterns on the bride's hands, the more her mother-in-law will love her.

All Sikhs, including the bride and groom, sit on the floor of the gurdwara during the marriage ceremony to show everyone is equal.

The marriage ceremony

Sikh weddings are generally held in the morning, in the gurdwara, or Sikh temple. They may also take place outdoors or in a marquee. As Sikhism is a religion of equals, there are no priests, and any Sikh man or woman can perform the marriage ceremony.

Wherever the marriage takes place, the groom is likely to arrive on horseback. The groom is often accompanied by a male relative who acts as his 'caretaker'.

The bride and groom are dressed in festive colours – he wears a turban (often in pink) and a scarf called a *pulla*. The bride wears a silk *shalwar kameez* (an outfit made up of a tunic worn over trousers), which may also be pink or another bright colour such as red or orange.

Before the religious ceremony, the families of the bride and groom greet each other, exchange gifts, and share snacks or tea in a milni, or meeting and welcoming ceremony.

Sikh men all over the world follow the northern Indian tradition of travelling to their wedding on horseback.

The couple then move into the temple and take their places on the floor, facing the Guru Granth Sahib, with the bride on the groom's left. Sikhs sit on the floor for all their worship, to show that everyone is equal and so no one is higher than the Guru Granth Sahib.

After making sure that both bride and groom understand and accept their responsibilities as Sikhs, and that they both fully agree to the marriage, the person conducting the ceremony talks about meaning of marriage and leads prayers, blessings and readings from the Guru Granth Sahib.

Sacred text

The sweetness of the beloved pervades our souls and bodies. God is dear to me and I to God on whom my mind is fixed day and night. By exalting God I have achieved my heart's desire. The beloved [God] has completed the union. The bride's mind has blossomed with the beloved's name. The beloved is united with the holy bride.

From the fourth Lavan, by Guru Ram Das

The bride and groom then promise to be faithful to each other, and one end of the groom's scarf is given to the bride to show that they are now joined. Now, connected both physically by the scarf and spiritually in marriage, the bride and groom walk four times around the Guru Granth Sahib. With each circuit, a verse of the Lavan, the Sikh wedding hymn, is sung.

At the end of the fourth round, the couple are showered with flowers and a sacred sweet pudding called *karah parshad* is shared by everyone. The wedding ceremony is complete, and married life begins.

A Sikh bride holds her groom's scarf to show they are joined as husband and wife.

Wedding celebrations

A wedding lunch follows the ceremony, and it is often served in the *langar*, the communal dining hall attached to every gurdwara.

Because many Sikhs are vegetarians, only vegetarian food is served. The langar is not just for celebrations. Free communal meals are served there every day, and they are an important part of Sikh life because they symbolize the Sikh principle of equality and sharing. To emphasize the fact that no one is above anyone else, everyone sits on the floor to eat.

After lunch, the bride changes into the clothes that her new in-laws have given her and gets ready to leave for her new home. This is often with her husband's family. The bride's departure is called *doli*, which refers to the traditional wedding procession in India, in which the bride is carried on a covered, decorated chair on poles. In modern Sikh weddings, especially in the West, the couple are more likely to leave in a decorated wedding car. As they go, the groom's father may shower the wedding car with coins to show his joy at the marriage.

That evening there is a doli dinner hosted by the groom's family for the couple and the bride's family.

Sikh weddings and after wedding lunches are held at the gurdwara. Only vegetarian food is served in the langar, which serves as an eating area for all members of the Sikh community.

This Sikh bride and groom are celebrating their wedding with a doli dinner. Doli dinners can be either small, quiet get-togethers with home cooked food, or large parties with singing and dancing.

The doli dinner may be a modest meal at the groom's parents' home, or it may be a more elaborate event held at a banqueting hall. The groom's family may also host a second wedding reception, either combined with the doli dinner or a few nights later, for the bride and groom's entire extended family. This may be a Western-style party, with dancing, where the bride and groom exchange rings and have a Western-style wedding cake.

When the bride arrives at her husband's house, she may find a pot of wheat or grain in the doorway. She will kick this over, spilling the grain inside the house, a symbolic gesture to show that she will bring food and prosperity to her new family. She may also remove her head covering or veil in the presence of the groom's female relatives, to show that she is now a member of their household.

FOCUS ON:
The bride's goodbye

Before she leaves the langar, the bride throws rice over her shoulder in four directions, to wish prosperity for the family she is leaving behind. Because she is now entering a new life, she must not look back at her old family. This can be one of the most emotional moments of a Sikh wedding, with tears shed by the bride and her family.

An equal partnership

*B*uddhists follow the teachings of Siddhattha Gotama, a prince who lived in India about 2,500 years ago. He became known as the Buddha, or 'enlightened one' when he achieved enlightenment after years of meditating and teaching about the meaning of life and why humans suffer.

This is a statue of Siddhattha Gotama, or the Buddha. The Buddha said, 'If a man can find a suitable and understanding wife and a woman can find a suitable and understanding husband, both are fortunate indeed'.

Buddhism neither encourages nor discourages marriage. Deciding whether or not to marry is based purely on personal choice. However, the Buddha taught that if people do marry, their marriage should be an equal partnership based on love and mutual respect. Husbands and wives, he said, should be loyal and provide for each other's needs. This would lead to a harmonious home and family life.

The Buddha did not impose any religious laws or commandments on his followers, so marriage is not seen as a spiritual duty or as a religious act. Therefore, Buddhist weddings follow the local customs and legal requirements of the community where they take place – there is no set Buddhist marriage service. Because there are Buddhist communities all over the world, there are many different kinds of Buddhist wedding.

Many Buddhists live in Southeast Asia, in countries where the general cultural practice is for parents to arrange marriages for their children. Families try to match partners on the basis of shared interests and family backgrounds.

When a Buddhist man decides he wants to marry, he first visits a Buddhist monk, or lama. The monk consults the groom's horoscope to discover a spiritually sound day to propose. The monk will also consult the horoscope of both the groom and bride-to-be to make sure that they are compatible for marriage. The horoscope is also checked to determine the most favourable day for the bride and groom to marry.

FOCUS ON:
Eightfold Path

Buddhists believe that following the Eightfold Path will lead to greater wisdom and goodness and less suffering in the world. For married couples, following the principles of the Eightfold Path will lead to a mutually respectful and harmonious marriage. The steps of the Eightfold Path are: 1. right view; 2. right intention; 3. right speech; 4. right action; 5. right livelihood; 6. right effort; 7. right mindfulness; 8. right concentration.

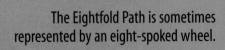

The Eightfold Path is sometimes represented by an eight-spoked wheel.

A Buddhist marriage

*A*lthough Buddhist marriages need not be religious, many Buddhist couples want their wedding to include elements of the Buddhist way of life that is so important to them. In Western countries, couples have a civil ceremony first, followed by a Buddhist blessing.

There are many different branches of Buddhism, all with slightly different traditions. Some Buddhist weddings, for example, are conducted by a male relative of the couple, and are followed with a blessing by a monk. The blessing may take place in a monastery, in a temple or at a shrine, before a statue of the Buddha under a covered canopy called a *purowa*.

A Buddhist couple light candles and incense at their wedding, to symbolize the enlightenment of the Buddha and the spread of his teachings.

On the day of the ceremony, the couple bring offerings of flowers to place before the Buddha. Lotus flowers are especially important in Buddhism because, although it has its roots in the mud, the lotus blossoms into a beautiful flower that faces the heavens. In the same way, Buddhists believe, people may be impure and rooted in the earth, but by following the principles of Buddhism they can strive for perfection.

With the couple seated before him, the monk chants from Buddhist scriptures known as *suttas*. Suttas are sometimes called sutras in English. The couple then recite the vows they have chosen, which may also be from the suttas.

A Buddhist monk pours water over the groom's hands to bring purity, clarity and calmness to his marriage.

After saying their vows, the couple exchange rings. Their parents may then say blessings for them, followed by those of the wedding guests. A ritual often included in Buddhist weddings is for the guests to pour water over the couple's hands as they bless them.

When the ceremony ends, the wedding party gathers for a festive meal. Because many Buddhists are vegetarians, meat is usually not served.

Sacred text

Buddhist couples are free to choose their own vows; many choose some version of these passages:

In five ways should a wife... be respected by a husband: by honouring, not disrespecting, being faithful, sharing authority, and by giving gifts.

And the wife so respected reciprocates with compassion in five ways: by being well-organized, being kindly disposed to the in-laws and household workers, being faithful, looking after the household goods, and being skilful and diligent in all duties.

From the Sigalovada Sutta, Digha Nikilya, 31

Hopi and Shinto weddings

The Native American Hopi nation have lived in their ancestral lands in northern Arizona in the United States for more than a thousand years, and still preserve many of their ancient beliefs and traditions. One of those beliefs is that marriage lasts not just for a lifetime, but into the afterlife as well.

FOCUS ON:
The wedding vase ceremony

During a Hopi wedding ceremony, the couple toast their union by drinking from a two-spouted vase. Tradition says that if they can both drink from the vase at the same time and not spill a drop, they will have a happy marriage.

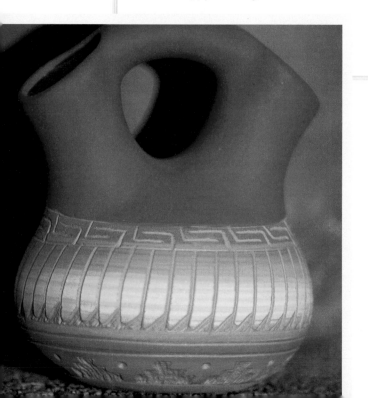

When a Hopi couple decides to marry, they tell first the bride's parents and then the groom's. The girl offers cornmeal or bread to her future mother-in-law. If she accepts the gift, the couple are considered engaged.

Corn is sacred to the Hopi, because of its fruitfulness and because it sustains life. The bride's family gives the groom's family two years of their corn harvest, as well as flour and corn cakes, to show they are skilled homemakers. In return, the groom's family weaves the bride's wedding clothes, and provides firewood and meat, to show that the groom will be a good provider.

Before sunrise on the morning of the wedding day, female relatives wash the bride and the groom's hair in a single basin, entwining strands of their hair to symbolize their lifelong union. The bride wears a white wedding robe with tassels at the corners to represent corn and fertility, and red stripes at the top and bottom. She will keep this all her life, and when she dies she will be buried in it. After a lengthy ceremony carried out by an elder of the community, the couple are married.

At the shrine the couple read their sacred vows, promising to be faithful to each other.

Shinto is one of the two main religions of Japan. Most Shinto weddings take place at a shrine. They are small, private events, shared only with the couple's close family and friends. The bride may wear a Western-style white wedding dress or a traditional white wedding kimono. The groom wears a traditional wedding outfit with a robe and wide, pleated trousers.

The priest first purifies the couple by pouring water over their hands, then waves branches to banish negative spirits. He blesses the couple and asks the *kami*, or gods, to protect them.

In a ceremony called *san-san-kudo* (meaning 'the way of three-three-nine'), the couple then share three cups of *sake* (rice wine) three times. Three is a lucky number in Japanese tradition, and nine – three times three – is particularly fortunate. Because odd numbers cannot be evenly divided, the san-san-kudo ceremony emphasizes that the married couple cannot be separated. The couple then exchange their vows and become husband and wife.

Sacred text

Bless them as unmoving and eternal. May their lives flourish like luxuriant trees. May they, bride and groom, together with heaven and earth, with the sun and the moon, continue to give out light and radiance.

Shinto marriage blessing

41

Celtic and African rituals

ecause marriage is such an important rite of passage, many people who are not religious and have a secular marriage still want to incorporate some form of ritual into their wedding day. They may create their own rituals and text, or they may borrow elements from various religions and cultures.

During a handfasting ceremony, a couple's hands are tied together. Some people believe that this is where the saying 'tying the knot', meaning to get married, came from.

A popular practice taken from the Celts of the Middle Ages, and still performed by neo-pagans or Wiccans, is the handfasting ceremony. The bride and groom's hands are bound together to symbolize their commitment to each other.

Handfasting was part of the standard marriage ceremony in ancient Rome, and was also done by the early Celts in Ireland and Scotland. When Ireland and Scotland became Christian, handfasting was done to mark a betrothal or 'trial marriage' that lasted a year and a day, or until the couple could have a church wedding.

Handfasting is becoming popular once more among couples in Ireland and Scotland, who may incorporate it into their civil wedding ceremony. On its own, it is not considered a legal form of marriage. Handfasting is now often used in same-sex marriages.

Another wedding custom that originated hundreds of years ago and is becoming popular again is 'jumping the broom', a practice that comes from West Africa. Among the Akan people in Ghana, brooms were seen as spiritually powerful and able to sweep away evil spirits. Brooms were waved over the heads of newlywed couples to assure them of a happy life together.

West Africans taken to America as slaves in the 17th to 19th centuries took many of their cultural beliefs and traditions with them. Slaves had no legal rights and could not marry, so slave couples devised their own marriage ceremonies, based on the traditions of their homeland. In front of witnesses, they made vows to one another then 'jumped the broom' to seal their marriage.

When slavery was abolished towards the end of the 19th century, the custom of jumping the broom was largely abandoned because of its associations with slavery. In recent years, however, many African-American couples have chosen to incorporate this ritual into their weddings as a way of honouring their ancestors and their heritage.

MODERN DEBATE:
SAME-SEX MARRIAGES

Same-sex partnership ceremonies are now legally recognized in some countries. People in these partnerships have the same rights and benefits as married couples. This has caused heated debate, especially in religious communities where same-sex partnerships are seen as a threat to morality and traditional family life. However, same-sex couples believe they should have the same right to marry as straight couples.

Do you think same-sex marriage should be allowed, or is it a threat to traditional family life?

Religion and marriage: a summary

Religion	Preparation	Marriage service
Christianity	Engagement with ring given to bride-to-be. Banns posted at parish churches of bride and groom.	Conducted by priest or minister. Bride wears white dress and veil. Service includes hymns and vows. May include Holy Communion. Rings exchanged.
Judaism	Ashkenazi grooms called to the Torah on the Sabbath before the wedding. Orthodox brides visit mikveh. Some Orthodox couples fast from sundown of the day before their wedding. Bride and groom sign ketubah before ceremony.	Conducted by rabbi. Bride wears white dress with veil. Groom wears kippah and tallit. Service includes Seven Blessings (Sheva Berakhot). Groom gives bride a ring. Groom stamps on glass at end of the ceremony.
Islam	Marriage may be arranged by families with consent of couple. Mehndi ceremony and party for decoration of bride's hands and feet.	Ceremony (the nikah) is conducted by imam or qazi, or by any respected Muslim man. Asian brides wear bright colours; North African and Middle Eastern brides usually wear white. Couple may sit separately, attended by guardians (walis).
Hinduism	Marriage may be arranged by families with couple's consent. Horoscopes consulted to ensure good match. Betrothal ceremonies at bride's, then groom's home. Betrothal rings exchanged. Mehndi ceremony at bride's house. Festive meal (sangeet) before the wedding. Milni (welcoming) just before wedding; tilak applied to groom's forehead.	Conducted by priest. Bride wears traditional sari. Groom wears traditional tunic, scarf and turban. Ceremony includes blessings, mantras, and circling the sacred fire four times. Groom's scarf and bride's sari tied in a marriage knot. Bride and groom recite vows.
Sikhism	Marriage traditionally arranged by parents with couple's consent. Engagement ceremony called shagun or kurmai held at groom's home. Mehndi night held for bride by women of both families.	Ceremony takes place in the morning. Groom wears turban and scarf; bride wears shalwar kameez. Ceremony conducted by a member of the community before the Guru Granth Sahib (holy book).
Buddhism	None prescribed; local customs are followed. In Asian countries, marriage may be arranged by couple's families.	May be conducted by a monk. May include candles, incense and chanting. Couple may recite vows and exchange rings.

Wedding venue	Gifts	Celebrations	After the wedding
Church	No specific practices. Gifts usually given to bride and groom at the reception.	Reception: a party, usually including a meal and dancing. Toasts made.	Couple go on honeymoon.
Under a canopy (chuppah), usually in a synagogue.	No specific practices. Gifts usually given to bride and groom at reception.	Reception: party and festive meal, usually with dancing. Bride and groom may be lifted into the air on chairs during dancing.	Relatives may hold a festive meal for the newlyweds on the seven evenings following the wedding. Couple then go on honeymoon.
Mosque, or bride or groom's home.	Groom gives bride gifts (mahar), usually before wedding. Gifts are given to bride and groom by guests at walima (marriage banquet). Bride's parents give groom gifts after the wedding.	Walima (marriage banquet) to announce wedding publicly and celebrate. Groom's family may host another meal a few days later.	Couple's wedding night may be spent in bride's parents' house, in separate rooms. Bride says goodbye to family (rukhsat); couple may go to live with groom's parents.
Canopy called a mandap – venue can be temple or hall.	At betrothal, bride given gifts by groom's mother. Sweets and gifts exchanged by families at milni. Groom's mother gives bride a mangla sutra (necklace) after ceremony. Family and friends give gifts at wedding feast.	Wedding feast.	Bride says farewell to her family, goes to home of in-laws, where she is welcomed by her mother-in-law.
Gurdwara, or outdoors in marquee.	At engagement ceremony, bride is given gifts by groom's family, and groom is given a kara (bracelet) and kirpan (sword) by bride's family.	Vegetarian wedding lunch in langar. Doli ('departure') dinner and reception hosted by groom's family.	Bride throws rice over her shoulders as she leaves for her in-laws' home, where she is welcomed as a new member of the household.
May be in a monastery, or at a temple or shrine.	No special practices.	Festive meal (usually vegetarian).	No special practices.

Glossary

altar in a Christian church, the table used for services such as Holy Communion

Anglican part of the Church of England

betrothal agreement between two people to get married

civil ceremony non-religious, legal marriage ceremony

dowry gift of money or property brought by a woman or her family to her husband, or to his family, when they get married

Eastern Orthodox the national churches of Greece, Russia, and some Slavic states, which grew out of a split between the two main centres of Christianity in the 11th century: Rome and Constantinople

engagement agreement between two people to get married

enlightenment in Buddhism a state of 'awakening', or understanding the true nature of the universe

ghee liquid part of butter that has been melted and chilled, so the liquid can be separated out

gurdwara Sikh place of worship

Guru teacher. In Sikhism, the title is used only for the first ten Sikh leaders and the Guru Granth Sahib.

halal anything that is lawful or permitted

henna dye made from the leaves of the henna plant mixed with ingredients such as tea or herbs to form a paste

Holy Communion sacrament in which bread and wine are taken as reminders of the last meal of Jesus Christ, and his death

karma force that results from someone's actions, and their consequences

kimono traditional Japanese dress

kosher literally 'fit' or 'proper', usually used to refer to food that complies with Jewish dietary laws

mantra a short, sacred Hindu text or prayer that is chanted or recited in repetition

meditation sitting quietly to clear the mind

mehndi henna used to paint designs on the bride's (and sometimes the groom's) hands and feet before their wedding

mosque Muslim place of worship

Orthodox Judaism Judaism in which the laws of the Torah are strictly followed

pagan follower of an ancient, nature-based religion such as Wicca

Protestant branch of Christianity that is separate from Roman Catholicism and Eastern Orthodoxy

Reform Judaism movement to modernize Jewish practice

reincarnation belief that after death a soul can be reborn in a different body

ritual set of actions performed in a particular way that is prescribed by a religion or tradition

Roman Catholic branch of Christianity that recognizes the Pope as its religious authority

Sabbath Jewish religious day of rest and worship

sacrament formal religious act that blesses the person or people performing it

sacred holy or worthy of religious respect

secular non-religious

synagogue Jewish place of worship

Find out more

Books

Facts about Religion: The Facts about Hinduism, Judaism, Christianity, Sikhism, Islam, Buddhism. Alison Cooper, (Wayland, 2004)

Religious Signs and Symbols: Judaism/Christianity/Hinduism/Islam. Cath Senker, (Wayland, 2008)

Sacred Texts: The Guru Granth Sahib and Sikhism. Anita Ganeri, (Evans, 2002)

The Lion Encyclopedia of Christianity. David Self, (Lion Hudson, 2007)

The Usborne Encyclopedia of Major World Religions. Susan Meredith and Clare Hickman, (Usborne, 2005)

World Faiths: Judaism. Trevor Barnes, (Kingfisher, 2005)

World Religions Today: Buddhism/Christianity. Kathryn Walker, (Wayland 2007)

World Religions Today: Hinduism/Islam/Judaism. Gianna Quaglia, (Wayland, 2007)

Websites

These websites offer comprehensive information about the six major world religions, plus many other faiths. In addition, each has links to numerous individual faith websites.

www.bbc.co.uk/religion/religions/

http://bible.beliefnet.com/index.html

www.religionfacts.com/

These websites have helpful information about rites of passage and marriage:

http://encarta.msn.com/encyclopedia_76155 7678_1____2/Rites_of_Passage.html

TEACHER NOTES

- Ask pupils to talk to married friends and relatives about their own weddings. What were their ceremonies like? What vows did they make?
- Look at photographs and videos of weddings. What ceremonies took place? What symbols can they see in the pictures?
- Ask pupils to write their own marriage vows – what promises would they include?
- Plan a visit to a nearby house of worship, and ask about how weddings are performed there. Ask to look at any ritual objects that might be used, as well as prayer books.

- Ask pupils to design wedding cards and/or wedding invitations for each of the religions studied. What symbols, words, and pictures will they include, and why?
- Ask pupils to list the similarities they find in marriage rituals of different religions. Why do they think these similarities exist?
- Ask pupils to think about their own lives, from birth until the present. What rites of passage have they already been through? Are there any events in their life that they think should have been marked as rites of passage? How would they have marked them?

Index